CHIC DECOR
DESIGN HOUSE

Making books beautiful.

Making books beautiful.

Explore other titles in the BEACH HOUSE SERIES

Create your own unique look by mixing and matching with popular titles from our other series:

PALM SPRINGS SERIES

DESIGNER BLACK&WHITE

BOLD LINEN SERIES

WOODLAND NATURE SERIES

Our design house would love to see how this book added beauty to your space.

We would be thankful if you could take a quick moment to leave your Amazon Review and if possible, include a photo of your unique creation using this Chic Decor Design House book.

Contact: chicdecordesignhouse@gmail.com